FOUNDER, ONLY A
PIT STOP

A Cinch To Fix Founder

HOOF
cinch

www.hoofcinch.com

CHUCK POTTER

ISBN 979-8-88943-917-2 (paperback)
ISBN 979-8-88943-918-9 (digital)

Christian Faith Publishing
832 Park Avenue
Meadville, PA 16335
www.christianfaithpublishing.com

Printed in the United States of America

HOOF ANATOMY

The hoof is a fantastic structure that deserves continual study by hoof-care professionals and anyone who owns a horse.

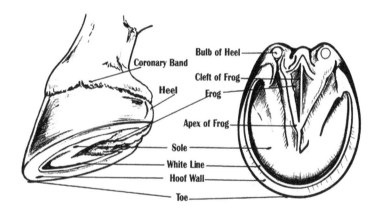

The hoof wall is produced by the coronary band. The hoof wall is comprised of two types of tubulars that run perpendicular to the ground. One tubular is hard, while the other is soft and is also the glue that holds the wall together. The unique nature of the tubulars allows the hoof wall to flex in every direction. Uneven weight bearing on the hoof wall will cause the wall to change shape and distort.

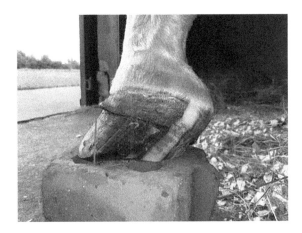

The distortion can easily be brought back into shape with proper trimming but may need a shorter trim cycle or shoeing to keep the wall from distorting again. During founder, the hoof wall can become distorted slightly due to the loss of the coffin bone attachment as the hoof wall is now more flexible without the bone support. Long slipper-looking hooves are not a sign of founder but instead a sign of neglect.

Outside of the tubulars is a coating called the periople. The periople grows down from the *periople* ring just above the coronary band but is usually worn off about a third of the way down the hoof wall. Often, during wet weather, the periople may appear as a white band just below the hairline on the hoof wall. Inside the hoof wall, the laminae attach the internal structures—the coffin bone and the lateral cartilages—to the hoof wall.

The sole and frog are the next two structures that have a sensitive and insensitive counterpart on the bottom of the hoof. The sole spreads the weight back to the hoof wall, and the frog acts as a last-chance shock absorber sending weight back to the sole and digital cushion. Both help protect the bones of the hoof.

The sole is a very good predictor of potential health issues since pigments will show in it as problems with the horse's thyroid, insulin levels, and pituitary gland begin.

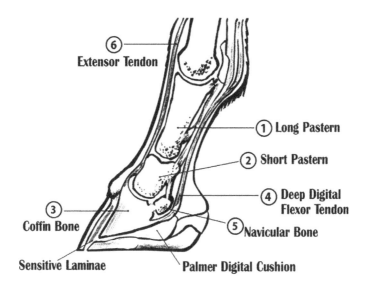

There are two tendons inside the hoof capsule. One is the extensor tendon, and the other is the deep digital flexor tendon. The extensor tendon runs down the front of the leg and ends at the extensor process on the top front part of the coffin bone. The deep digital flexor tendon is in the back of the leg and ends on the bottom of the coffin bone after passing over the navicular bone.

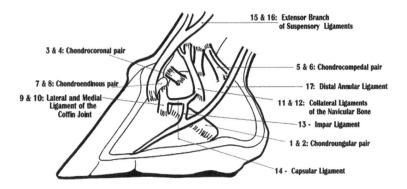

There are seventeen ligaments in the hoof:

Four pairs attach the collateral ligament to the bones in the hoof.

- 1 and 2—The chondroungular pair attach to the coffin bone.
- 3 and 4—The chondrocoronal pair attach to the short pastern.
- 5 and 6—The chondrocompedal pair attach to the long pastern.
- 7 and 8—The chondroendimous pair attach to the extensor tendon as it attaches to the extensor process.
- 9 and 10—The lateral and medial ligaments of the coffin joint attach the coffin bone to the short pastern.
- 11 and 12—The collateral ligaments of the navicular bone attach the navicular bone to the long pastern.
- 13—The impar ligament attaches the coffin bone to the navicular bone.
- 14—The capsular ligament of the coffin joint contains and provides synovial fluid.
- 15 and 16—The extensor branch of suspensory ligaments attaches to the extensor tendon as it attaches to the extensor process of the coffin bone.
- 17—The distal annular ligament circles the deep flexor as it enters the hoof.

There are two bones in the hoof and one partially in the hoof.

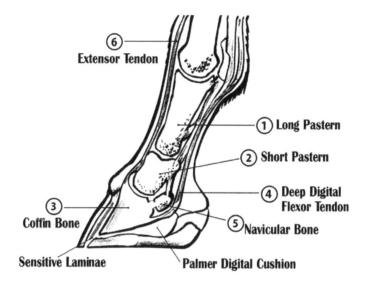

The two bones inside the hoof are the coffin bone (P-3) and the navicular bone. The coffin bone is generally the shape of the hoof wall and is attached to the hoof wall via the laminae. The coffin bone is the only bone in the horse's body that does not have a periosteum (bone sheath). The two collateral cartilages attach to the wings of the coffin bone and allow the heels to expand and contract as well as help circulate blood in the venous plexus. The navicular bone is a sesamoid that is under the short pastern and coffin bone joint. A sesamoid acts as a pivot point and glide for a tendon. The navicular bone allows the deep digital flexor tendon to change direction and glide smoothly as the horse moves its hoof. The bone that is partially in the hoof is called the short pastern (P-2).

Blood flow for the hoof is not as complicated as it seems. The blood travels through the digital arteries down the back of the horse's leg until it gets to the fetlock and then moves to the rear sides of the lower leg before entering the hoof near the heels.

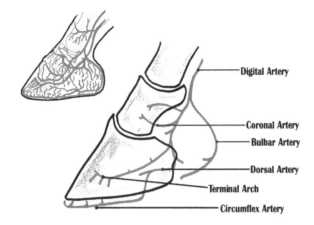

Digital Artery

Coronal Artery

Bulbar Artery

Dorsal Artery

Terminal Arch

Circumflex Artery

The digital artery feeds the coronal artery, bulbar artery, para-cuneal artery, circumflex artery, terminal arch, dorsal arteries, and palmer arteries. Each digital artery can supply the entire hoof with the blood flow needed to stay healthy. The blood is circulated back up the leg via the digital veins to the lungs to be resupplied with oxygen. The blood circulates in the hoof because of the heart of the animal and not because of movement or pressure on the frog of the hoof. Movement and pressure can help move oxygen and other gases from the soft tissue or blood vessels to one another via the venous plexus, but the circulation will occur even if the animal is lying down with its hooves up on the coffee table watching TV.

There are many misconceptions about the blood circulation in the hoof capsule, and these falsities run rampant through the horse community. We try to equate what we know about blood flow in the toenails of animals we are more familiar with, such as dogs, to that of a horse.

As a dog's toenails become long, the quick become longer over time, and it is easier to make the toenail bleed when trimming it. This is not the case with the long or neglected horse's hoof. The blood vessels stay where they are supposed to be and do not become longer or move away from the bones. Therefore, we can take a severely neglected hoof and trim it back to normal in one trimming without fear of hitting an artery or blood vessel. When a hoof is long and neglected, it needs to be trimmed back to normal as quickly as possible to relieve the extra stresses it is causing on the rest of the animal's legs.

Trimming a little at a time is the ignorance of an untrained *farrier* who is scared to trim the hoof properly because he or she does not know where the internal structures are. During founder, the blood vessels stay with the bones and continue to supply the damaged laminae. Another misconception is that the blood flow can be restricted by applying pressure to the hoof wall with the Hoof Cinch. The Hoof Cinch is attached to the hoof wall directly and therefore cannot restrict any blood circulation.

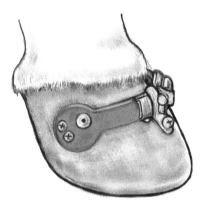

Hoof Cinch

The Cinch is only able to stop the flex of the front of the hoof capsule and redirect the growth of the new horn as it comes in. If the band was connected to an external device, such as a shoe, then it would be possible to restrict some blood flow in the dorsal aspect of the hoof capsule (front of the hoof).

LAMINITIS

What is laminitis?

Laminitis and founder are often used incorrectly and interchange-ably, even though they are two different conditions. Laminitis is an inflammation or irritation of the laminae. The laminae attach the hoof wall and coffin bone.

Founder is when the coffin bone rotates or sinks away from the hoof wall. Instead of letting go of the bone or hoof wall when the rotation happens, the laminae will stretch as the bone moves away from the hoof wall.

Signs

Horses become lame when they have laminitis. Laminitis is usu-ally found in the front hooves, but all four can be affected. About 60 percent of the horse's body weight is over its front feet, so there will be more damage where there is more weight. In the initial stages of laminitis, the horse can show symptoms of a minor limp, but when resting and moving, there will be a noticeable shift in weight to the hind legs and hooves.

Usually, the horse will be fairly inactive and will want to lie down to relieve some pain. The gums of the horse may also be red, and the digital pulse will be rapid and strong.

Causes

While there are many causes of laminitis, some are speculative while others are known to be factual. Factual reasons for laminitis are as follows:

1. grain overload
2. insulin resistance (IR) or equine metabolic syndrome (EMS) (insulin levels are high)
3. elevated levels of ACTH, which is a hormone produced by the pituitary gland (insulin levels may be high)
4. some tick-borne diseases
5. equine protozoal myeloencephalitis (EPM)
6. black walnut ingestion.
7. Potomac fever

Laminitis is a serious condition that must be managed as quickly as possible. Horse owners should remove the horse from all probable causes of laminitis and call their vet and farrier. The horse should be kept in a stall or dry lot that has no food, other than grass hay, or supplements available until diagnosis. If the horse is unable to stand, a feed muzzle can keep him from eating the surrounding grasses. Allow the vet to draw blood to determine the causes of the laminitis. The farrier should apply the Hoof Cinch and trim to increase the angles of the hoof if possible. Sometimes, wedge shoes may be applied to elevate the heels.

This will reduce the pull of the deep digital flexor tendon and help reduce the chances of rotation. The horse may be administered pain and anti-inflammatory medications to reduce swelling and relieve some of the pain.

FOUNDER

Founder is the movement of the coffin bone away from its normal position. The bone can rotate downward, slide downward along the hoof wall, or do both at once.

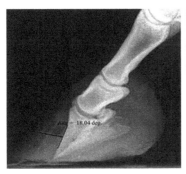 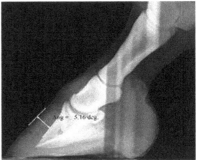

The signs will be similar to laminitis, but the horse will usually demonstrate more lameness or even immobility. The digital pulse will be strong and rapid, and there will be heat in the front of the affected hooves. X-rays and blood tests are usually necessary to confirm founder. The cause of founder must be stopped, or the horse may not survive. Apply the Hoof Cinch as soon as possible and elevate the heels. Make sure the soles are not touching the ground as the horse bears weight, as sole pressure will cause great discomfort and bone demineralization.

Founder prevention

Preventing founder has been said to be easy, but if this were the case, there would not be more than one million foundered horses in the United States each year.

Many causes of founder are environmental. Certain grasses, black walnut, and other weeds make it difficult for horse owners to keep their horse safe from founder.

Unfortunately, some breeds of horses are more prone to founder and laminitis than others. Paso Fino, Morgan, and Tennessee walking horses are just a few breeds that are more likely to founder. These breeds need extra care in feeding, proper pasture maintenance, weight management, and general care. However, no breed is exempt, and each horse owner should take these precautions.

No matter what the cause of the horse's founder, it is important to know how to prevent laminitis and founder.

A horse's diet that the owner can control is the best place to start in preventing founder.

Most horses need little more than good grass hay, a salt lick, and a mineral block. Letting horses graze in lush pastures for hours is never a good idea. Although horses are designed to eat grass all day, domestic horses usually do not get enough exercise to be able to handle continual grazing.

If the horse in question is a pasture pet, feeding it the correct diet in the right amount is very important. Horses that are worked and stay more active also need to be fed the correct diet in the right amounts. Feeding the horse by its size, workload, systemic issues, and body type can save the horse and owner the pain and misery of dealing with laminitis and founder.

Horse owners have a tendency to equate their wants and need to those of our equine friends. One example is feeding extra grain during colder days to keep the horse warm or putting a blanket on the horse.

These things make us feel better but do very little for the comfort of the horse. This has undesired effects on horses. Horses that are overweight with metabolic issues often develop other serious medical problems. Symptoms that may indicate your equine friend is heading for problems are being overweight, acting sluggish, displaying stiff movements, having changes in coat, having pigments in the soles of the hooves, having attitude changes, and displaying fatigue.

Treatments

Fixing the mechanical part of founder is the easiest part of the process. Finding the underlying cause is almost always the hardest part. To treat a foundered horse, the sole pressure needs to be cleared, the angle of the hoof needs to be increased, and the Hoof Cinch should be applied.

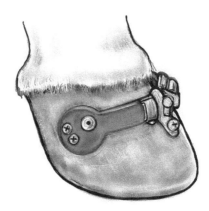

Hoof Cinch

Some horses will need to be shod to either (a) get their soles off the ground so the tip of the coffin bone is not being subjected to ground pressure or (b) provide support to the column of the leg and hoof if there is sinking involved.

If there is a sinking of the coffin bone, a boney column support system needs to be used. The type of frog support will depend on what the horse can tolerate having done as well as the ability of the farrier and condition of the hooves.

The heart bar shoe is the best boney column support system as it supports the hoof wall and frog while leaving sole pressure clear. It does take a farrier who is trained to properly apply the heart bar shoe so that it is effective. The treatment for the underlying cause will depend on the cause of the laminitis. Talk with a qualified equine veterinarian for the best treatment options. Testing the horse for the cause of founder is very important to do early on. Instead of waiting until the horse can no longer walk, contact a farrier and vet as soon as symptoms appear.

People often look for instant gratification, but unfortunately, making continual changes in vitamins, minerals, drugs, and diet is detrimental to a foundering horse.

Since the horse's system has failed for one reason or the other, continual changes in the diet will continue to stress the horse's system.

Natural methods will sound appealing during this time, but they may cause the horse to suffer for months or even years later. Luckily, there are medications and mechanical devices that can make the horse more comfortable and help them recover quicker.

Unfortunately, many methods taught to farriers and vets for helping a foundered horse do more damage than good. One method that is commonly used, but is never good for a foundering horse, is lowering the heels to get the frog on the ground or attempting to realign the three lower bones.

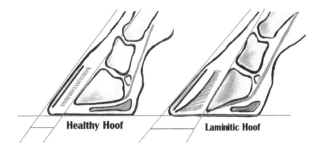

Healthy Hoof   Laminitic Hoof

When these methods are used on a foundering horse, the tension on the deep digital flexor tendon is increased, so the coffin bone is pulled in a downward motion against the already failing laminae. Forces pushing up through the sole are never helpful during laminitis or founder. A heart bar shoe can be used if the coffin bone is sinking, but it must be applied correctly.

Applying a reverse shoe is another incorrect method.

Farriers and vets are taught that a reverse shoe removes the pressure from the front of the hoof, but it actually increases the pressure on the front of the hoof wall. The entire hoof capsule needs to be in contact with the ground surface to dissipate the weight that the coffin bone is transmitting through the laminae to the hoof capsule.

If a shoe is needed, it is best to use an open-heeled wedge shoe.

This will remove ground forces from injuring the coffin bone further and decrease the pull of the deep digital flexor tendon. A regular wedge shoe supports the entire hoof wall and gives the horse a mechanical advantage.

A rocker shoe is another example of a shoe that should not be applied. It may cause additional problems because the internal structures are unstable due to the failure of the laminae.

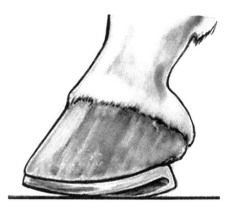

A destabilizing external structure applied to that failed system is not helpful.

HOOF CINCH

Vet and farrier schools teach that founder cannot be cured. This was true before the invention of the Hoof Cinch.

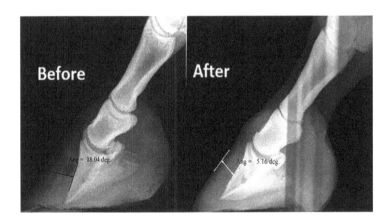

The Hoof Cinch stabilizes the front of the hoof wall to reduce the increased flexibility of the front of the hoof wall due to laminae failure and bone attachment loss. This can help to relieve the pain of the stretched laminae and start the new hoof wall growing down from the coronary band to be redirected back toward the coffin bone. The Hoof Cinch will work on acute to chronic cases of founder.

The Hoof Cinch was tested on sixty horses over a period of one year. Thirty foundered horses were treated with twenty-nine recoveries. The other thirty were a mix of normal horse and horses with ringbone, sidebone, navicular, and other undiagnosed hoof pains. The Hoof Cinch only works on laminitic and foundered horses. It will realign the hoof wall to the bone, even in cases that have happened years ago. Horses that are sound but still have old rotations can still be fixed. It did not make any changes or do any damage to the non-foundered horses that were tested.

BARN TALK

Barn talk is a source of great misinformation. Many wives' tales are circulated that make it tough for the farrier and vet to keep the horse owner correctly informed. The vet and farrier have a plan set up for the horse.

Often, the owner decides it is best to talk with the barn owner, who is "far more knowledgeable" than the vet and farrier, and together they decide it is best to add a little feed, supplements, and exercise. The farrier returns on schedule to find the horse still not doing well but is not told of the "enhanced treatments" that the owner and her friend decided to add. Weeks later, the vet is called back to the barn as the horse is getting worse. The vet and the farrier do a little questioning and finally find out that their plan was "enhanced" by the owner and friend.

This happens more often than I care to recount.

Horse owners should be able to trust what their farrier or vet tells them, but unfortunately, their knowledge may be incorrect if they were not taught properly. In the United States, there are no standards in the horse world that guarantee anyone is an expert. Even in universities and colleges, a lot of misinformation is taught. Anyone can pick up tools and call him or herself a farrier—without so much as going to a clinic or a trade school.

Oftentimes, vets are not well trained on the subject of the horse's hoof; they gain more knowledge by working with whatever farrier happens to be in their area, reading a book, or attending a clinic. The horse owner is left to decide what is right and what is wrong. The problem is that there are so many theories and practices in the horse world—school-trained farriers, club-trained farriers, two-day-clinic farriers, barefoot farriers, natural, blacksmith, certified, accredited, and many more farriers of different backgrounds. Most of them try to convince horse owners that their approach is the best.

Horses are amazing animals and can survive horrible injuries. Owners, farriers, and vets have to give the horse the best chance to recover by doing what is best for the horse.

Every horse is different, so one method will not work the same way on all horses. Farriers must have many options so that if their primary option doesn't work, they can have alternative plans ready.

The most common problem farriers and vets face is a noncompliant horse owner. A noncompliant owner can sabotage the work of the farrier and vet. It is sometimes necessary to remove the horse from the owner's control in order to ensure recovery. Some problems are unavoidable, such as not having a stall or a way to sequester the horse to a dry lot. Other problems can occur when owners neglect to give their horse medications or continue to let their horse graze on lush green pastures.

The vet and the farrier must lay out exactly what needs to be done to help the horse and ask the owner if the treatment plan can be accomplished. If it is not possible, the team needs to come up with alternative methods to help the horse.

Farriers become frustrated when they have to keep returning to a horse that is not making progress, only to find out that the horse is being given supplements or vitamins that the owner has read about online.

Owning a foundered horse is not always easy. There must be a commitment by the owner, farrier, and vet to keep the horse sound. The owner has the biggest responsibility to make sure the horse is being kept in an environment that is safe for the horse: eating only what it can safely digest, getting the correct medicine, and being kept on an appropriate trimming cycle. Most foundered horses can stay on a trim cycle of five to eight weeks.

Whether to shoe the horse or not is decided using several factors. The farrier will need to consider whether he can get the soles cleared with trimming so the horse is not walking directly on its soles. The farrier may need to consider how close the bone is to the bottom of the soles, if the bone is sinking, and whether or not the horse normally wears shoes.

If shoes are needed, then the farrier has to decide which type of shoes to apply. The farrier must decide whether the horse can handle the pain of hammering and determine what kind of surface the horse is living on. Most foundered horses can go barefoot if trimmed properly. The heels should be elevated, and the toe should be trimmed back and up, as long as the sole depth will allow it. Under no circumstance should the horse be walking directly on its soles. The horse will suffer needlessly with improper trimming. If the dead sole cannot be safely removed, then a shoe should be applied to get the sole off the ground. If the horse can tolerate the hammering, then a 2.5-degree open-heeled wedge shoe should be applied. If the horse cannot tolerate the hammering, then there are several options available. Many types of glue-on shoes are available today. Pads should be used with caution as they harbor bacteria and may cause abscesses that are dangerous for a foundering horse.

If the coffin bone is sinking, a frog support system needs to be applied. There are many options, and the best is to apply the heart bar shoe. Only a trained farrier, who has been taught how to properly apply the shoe, should apply the heart bar, as it can cause damage if improperly applied.

The forces on the lower leg and hoof are affected by what is done to the hoof internally and externally. The farrier affects the forces by the angle of the trim and how shoes are applied. The lower the angle that the hoof is trimmed, the greater the forces will be on the hoof, both internally and externally. For the purpose of explaining the forces on the leg, we made some generalizations about the balance of the horse as he stands square.

These are not made to show an accurate depiction of weight distribution but rather to show how angles and shoe placement cause changes in the forces on the leg.

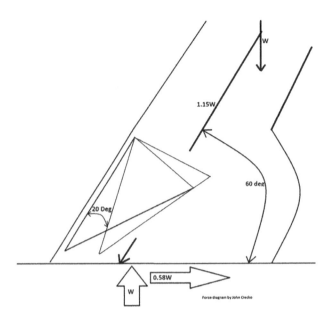

Force diagram by John Ciecko

If you look at the diagram of the forces, you can see that force exerted on the hoof capsule is 0.15 greater than on the downward force of the upper leg. If the angle of the trim is lowered, then the force becomes greater. The reason we discuss this is to show that when there is an internal problem, such as founder, lowering the angles will increase the stresses on the already injured and failing structures. There are several different forces working on different parts of the hoof at the same time.

There will be a downward force from the horse's weight, an upward force due to ground contact, and a friction force that keeps the horse's foot from sliding forward. The bottom of the hoof is shown as a circle for the distribution of weight calculations. If a part of the circle is changed as to what part contacts the ground, then the force distribution is changed. If we place a shoe on the hoof backward so that the front hoof wall is no longer supported, it will seem that we have reduced the forces on the front of the hoof wall, but this is not the case.

You have now increased the forces that the sole in the front of the hoof must support, and the laminae are under greater stress due to a fanning forward pressure of the increased weight to the back of the hoof wall.

As you can see, this is bad for a foundering horse. The increase in pressure on the coffin bone will create a point pressure at the tip of the coffin bone. These pressures also affect the deep digital flexor tendon and the extensor tendon. During a founder episode, the laminae are a failing system. By increasing the angle and supporting the hoof wall, with trimming or shoeing, we can decrease the forces to the failing area in the front of the hoof wall.

Treatment methods must address the changing pressures to allow the healing of the laminae. Increasing the angle and supporting the hoof wall, either with trimming or shoeing, can decrease the forces on the failing area in the front of the hoof wall. The Hoof Cinch replaces the tensile strength that was lost at the front of the hoof wall. This allows the hoof wall and coffin bone to return to a more normal alignment and reduces or eliminates the imposed tension on the laminae, thereby giving the hoof time to time to heal.

Horses are great survivors despite what people decide is best for them.

Most foundering horses will survive even if the wrong things are done to them, but they need not suffer for months or years anymore. The Hoof Cinch, along with proper diagnosis and medical treatment, can make for a quick and less painful recovery.

ABOUT THE AUTHOR

Chuck Potter's wide-ranging experience helps him look at problems from many different angles. He spent twenty years working in US Special Forces and military intelligence, and in addition to doing bodyguard work in hostile areas, he has facilitated communications systems, working in countries as diverse as Egypt, Japan, the Philippines, Vanuatu, Iraq, Australia, Germany, Kazakhstan, Uzbekistan, Afghanistan, Jordan, Germany, Austria, Switzerland, and Sweden. He holds an associate's degree in computer programming and technology from Pierce College and a BS in equine studies from Post College. He is a graduate of the Minnesota School of Horseshoeing. Potter studies problems and forms solutions that are effective and safe while also keeping the horse and owner a central focus. His ability to combine farrier science with new concepts has resulted in patents for devices that save many horses around the world.